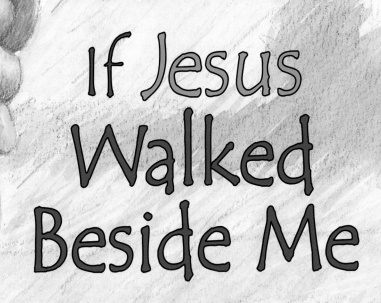

If Jesus Walked Beside Me

Written by
Jill Roman Lord

Illustrated by
Renée Graef

ideals children's books.

Nashville, Tennessee

ISBN-13: 978-0-8249-5625-7

Published by Ideals Children's Books
An imprint of Ideals Publications
A Guideposts Company
Nashville, Tennessee
www.idealsbooks.com

Text copyright © 2006 by Jill Roman Lord
Art copyright © 2006 by Ideals Publications

Color separations by Precision Color Graphics, Franklin, Wisconsin

Printed and bound in Italy

Library of Congress Cataloging-in-Publication Data

Lord, Jill Roman.
  If Jesus walked beside me / written by Jill Roman Lord ;
illustrated by Renée Graef.
    p. cm.
            alk. paper
  1. Jesus Christ—Presence—Juvenile literature. I. Graef, Renée.
II. Title.

BT590.P75L67 2005
242'.62—dc22

                                    2005013917

Lego_Jun10_1

For Abby, Emily, and Jonathon

If Jesus walked beside me,
Then I'd grow so brave and strong.
I'd feel his peace and comfort and
His presence all day long.

And when I'd hear the coach say, "Swing!"
When I stood up at bat,
If Jesus walked beside me,
Then I'd not be scared of that.

I'd turn my eyes to Jesus, who'd say,
"Do the best you can."
I'd hit the ball so hard, it'd fly
To China or Japan!

He'd help me ride my brand-new bike,
The one that made me fall.
He'd say, "Now, you can do it, friend.
Believe you can!" he'd call.

I'd rocket past the square in town
And never once fall down.
I'd look to Jesus, hold on tight,
And zip on through the town.

If other children called me names,
I wouldn't run away.
I'd turn to meet them face-to-face,
And this is what I'd say:

"It's time you met my greatest friend,
Who helps me all day through.
If you'd take Jesus as your friend,
He'd do the same for you."

On days when I'd feel very sick,
Too ill to run and play,
I'd cling to Jesus by my side.
He'd hold me through the day.

I'd feel his peace and comfort as
His hand brushed through my hair.
I'd sense a joy from deep inside,
Just knowing he was there.

If Jesus walked beside me through
A gusty wind or storm,
I wouldn't shake and tremble, 'cause
He'd keep me safe and warm.

I just can't get that figure eight,
No matter how I try.
With Jesus here to comfort me,
I wouldn't even cry!

He'd say, "I want to hear your cares,
Your problems and concerns.
Together we will make it through
Life's toughest twists and turns."

At night I'd snuggle into bed,
Beneath the moonlit glow.
I'd give a hug to Jesus, and
I'd wish he'd never go.

He'd say, "I'm always by your side
To guide you through your day.
I always hear you when you call.
I'm just a prayer away."

If Jesus walked beside me, I
Have told you what I'd do.
Now tell me what you'll do if . . .

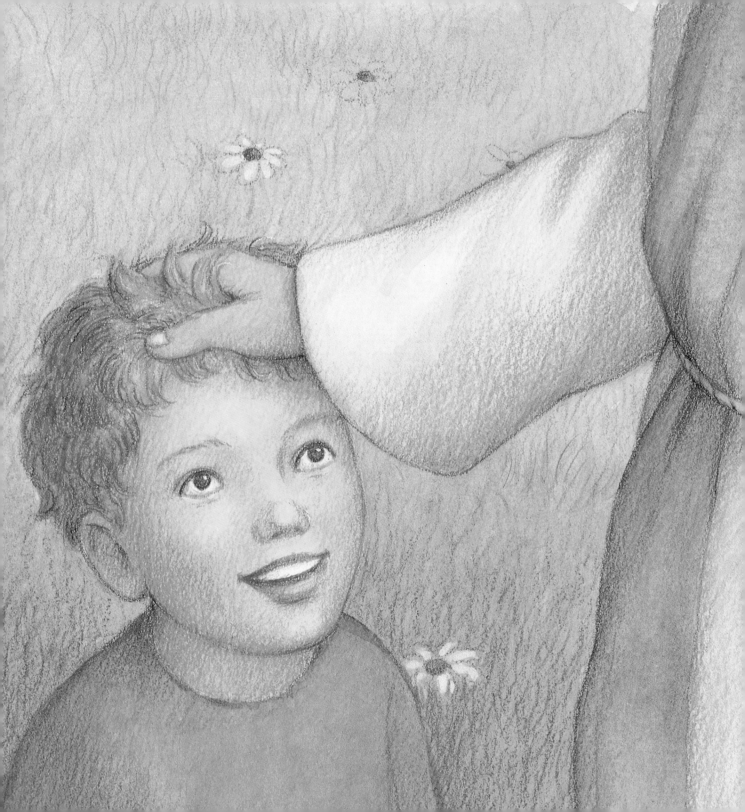

Someday he walks with you?